This book belongs to:

....

....

LET'S
TALK

Daddy's getting married

Written by Jennifer Moore-Mallinos

Illustrated by Marta Fàbrega

SALARIYA
BH
BOOK HOUSE

When my parents got divorced and Daddy moved to a different house, it took me a little while to get used to things.

4

At first I was so angry and
upset that Daddy had moved away
that I didn't want to talk to him. When
Daddy came to pick me up for a visit,
I would cry and scream and make a fuss.
I suppose I thought that if I acted badly, Mum
and Dad would become friends again.

Then, on one of my days with Daddy, he told me that he had a new friend that he wanted me to meet. Before I could say NO, she showed up! Not only did I refuse to say hello to her, but I spilled my drink on purpose and didn't even help clean up the mess. Instead, I sat with my arms folded and made a really horrible face at her!

Daddy's friend must have really liked him, because no matter how badly I acted and no matter how hard I tried, she wouldn't go away; instead, she was nice to me! Daddy kept telling me that even with a new friend, nothing would ever change and that he would always be there for me, no matter what.

He was right! I talk to Daddy every day on the phone and I visit his house every week. Whenever there's a special occasion, Daddy comes over to my house to help us celebrate. We always have so much fun together that sometimes I forget that Daddy has to leave to go to his own house at the end of the night. I always feel a little sad when he goes.

But then things started to change. Whenever I went to Daddy's house for a visit, his friend was always there. I never seemed to have Daddy all to myself any more! Even though Daddy's friend is pretty (but not as pretty as Mum), and she's really nice to me, especially when she helps me with my maths homework, I still miss being a family with just Mum and Dad.

Sometimes, when I'm all alone, I dream that Mum and Dad will become best friends again and I wonder what it would be like if we were all together as a family, just like before. Maybe if Daddy hadn't found a new friend things would be different. But Daddy did meet a new friend, and now he's getting married!

When my parents told me that Daddy was getting married, I couldn't believe it! I was shocked. I felt sad that my dreams of becoming a family again were never going to come true. Another part of me was cross with Daddy for not giving me and Mummy another chance. I was confused and I didn't know how or what I was supposed to feel. Mum and Dad both gave me a big hug and promised that nobody could ever take their place as my parents, no matter what!

It took a while for me to really believe that Daddy was getting married. When he asked me to be a flower girl at his wedding and asked if I could help with some of the wedding plans, I didn't know what to say. I was worried about Mummy and I didn't want to hurt her feelings by being at Daddy's wedding, but I knew I didn't want to say NO either. What was I going to do?

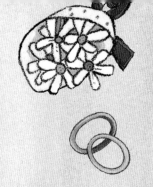

That's when I decided that the best thing to do was to talk to Mum. So I told her how confused I felt and how I wished she was getting married to Daddy so we could be a family again. Mum said it was all right for me to feel this way and even though Dad was getting married, we would always be a family and nobody could ever take that away.

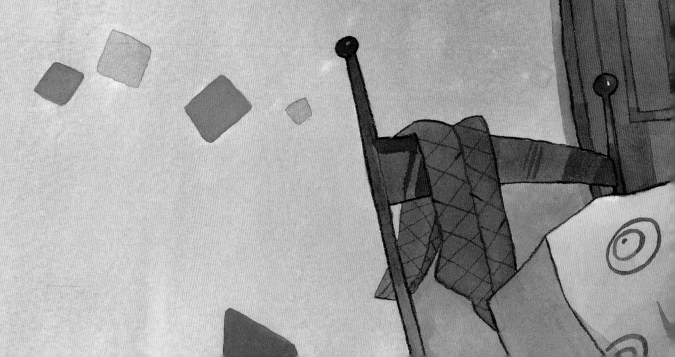

Daddy was so happy that I wanted to be part of his special day. The only thing I still wasn't sure about was what I was supposed to call Daddy's friend. It didn't feel right calling her 'Mum' because I already had a Mum, and I didn't want to call her 'Auntie' because she's not my Aunt. So we all decided that it was OK for me to call Daddy's friend by her first name, Cindy.

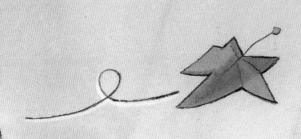

Planning the wedding took up most of
Daddy's time and, even though I had
fun choosing my dress and my flowers,
I sometimes felt a little left out.

It seemed like all Daddy worried about was the wedding and what Cindy wanted. I couldn't wait for the wedding to be over, because maybe then things would go back to normal.

When the big day finally came I was so excited! I felt really special all dressed up with my fancy hairdo and big bouquet of flowers.

I smiled for all the photographs, just as I promised I would, and when it was my turn to dance with Daddy, he gave me the biggest hug ever, then told me he loved me. That's when I knew that everything was going to be OK!

After the wedding, everything seemed to go back to normal. I talk to Daddy as much as I want to on the phone, and I visit his house every week. On special occasions Cindy and Daddy come over to my house to help me and Mum celebrate. Even Mummy and Cindy have become friends. When I'm alone, I think of the family I have now and I feel happy. Mum and Dad will always be my parents and nobody could ever replace them, but it's nice having Cindy around, especially since she's really good at maths! And guess what? Mum has a new friend now, too!

Note to Parents

Daddy's getting married acknowledges the reality of many families in today's society. It explores some of the anxieties and concerns your children may experience during the changes within your family when either parent remarries. When children are allowed the opportunity to explore their thoughts, feelings (both good and bad) and even their fears, they will not only feel validated as important members of your family, but they will be reminded that their feelings matter.

This book can be used as an interactive tool to initiate dialogue and stimulate communication between you and your child. *Daddy's getting married* is geared to assist you and your child in taking an important step towards a new and happy family.

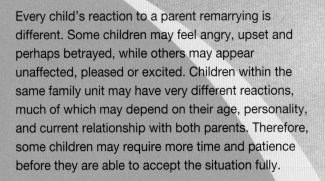

Every child's reaction to a parent remarrying is different. Some children may feel angry, upset and perhaps betrayed, while others may appear unaffected, pleased or excited. Children within the same family unit may have very different reactions, much of which may depend on their age, personality, and current relationship with both parents. Therefore, some children may require more time and patience before they are able to accept the situation fully.

If your child seems to be having a difficult time in coming to terms with the situation and appears 'stuck' in his or her ability to move forward in a positive way, you may want to consult your family doctor for advice.

There are many ways to interact with your child, all of which are important. Taking the time to read this book to your child is not only a great way to share a moment together, but it allows you an opportunity to focus your interaction on a specific topic.

As you read through this book, encourage your children to share their thoughts and feelings and to ask questions. Most importantly, provide them with a comfortable, stress-free environment for this to happen. Your understanding and patience will not go unnoticed!

Published in Great Britain in
MMXIII by Book House, an imprint of
The Salariya Book Company Ltd
25 Marlborough Place, Brighton BN1 1UB
www.salariya.com
www.book-house.co.uk

1 3 5 7 9 8 6 4 2

A CIP catalogue record for this book is available
from the British Library.

Printed and bound in China.

PB ISBN: 978-1-908973-25-2

Original title of the book in Spanish: Mi papá se casa
© Copyright MMVI by Gemser Publications, S.L.
El Castell, 38; Teià (08329) Barcelona, Spain (World Rights)

Other titles in this series:
My friend has Down's syndrome
I remember
Lost and found
Have you got a secret?
Colours of the rainbow
When my parents forgot how to be friends
My brother is autistic

Visit our **new** online shop at
shop.salariya.com
for great offers, gift ideas, all our new
releases and free postage and packaging.